Listen
with your
whole
self

MAURA VAUGHN

stillpoint/athena

Stillpoint/Athena
Stillpoint Digital Press
stillpointdigitalpress.com
Mill Valley California

ISBN 978-1-938808-42-5

PLEASE

Write
thank you notes

Handwrite them
if possible

Respond
to invitations
even if you can't go

Answer emails promptly

Read emails all the way through twice

Never respond
in anger

Wait to press send

Be patient
with yourself
and with others

Hold doors open for people

All people

Never allow
expediency
to be an
excuse for
discourtesy

Say what worked before you launch into what didn't

Listen
with your
whole
self

Don't agree
to something
unless you are
clear what
you are
agreeing to

Live up
to your
agreements

Do things
for others

You'll like
yourself more

Be kind

Give people enough time to be prepared

Everyone wants to do their best

Play well
with others

Share

Even the spotlight

Win-Win
is the best
result

Hold yourself
in regard
and to
the highest
standard

Treat everyone with
the same regard
you would like
to be shown

Give yourself
enough time
to get
where you are going

That way you keep
everyone safe

Stay healthy
everyone needs you
at your best

Work hard
but get enough sleep

Own up to your mistakes

Celebrate the accomplishments of others

Celebrate your failures

Often they teach you more than your successes

Speak with integrity

Gossip only hurts your own reputation

Practice empathy
You will be grateful
you did

Forgive people

Even yourself

Apologize

Lend a hand
whenever you can

Clean up
after yourself

It says nice things
about you

Read
instructions
carefully

Read
the ingredients
before starting
the recipe

Recycle

Waste
is a sad
reflection
on our culture

VOTE

THANK YOU